The
Freshman
15

ISBN: 978-0-9974817-5-4

The Freshman 15

a 15-week devotional for a
freshman's first semester in college

Tommy McGregor

Table Of Contents

Introduction

The term "Freshman 15" is synonymous with physical health. If you are unfamiliar with the phrase, it exists under the assumption that a typical freshman goes to college and gains 15 pounds while experiencing the bliss of unlimited freedom (and a lot of late night pizza). Who knows if it is actually true? Obviously it is not guaranteed, but the concept is based on a common reality.

College is a time of endless opportunities. Some of these experiences will help you create lasting memories, while others might cause you to buy larger waisted pants.

I have always thought that the Freshman 15 concept could represent even more than physical health. A mismanagement of freedom in college can lead to unhealthy relationships, poor grades, and a immature faith that causes you to lose more than the 15 pounds of weight you might gain.

This devotional book is an opportunity to help you re-balance your life as you deal with the real-time challenges associated with your transition to this new stage of life. In these pages, you will find 15 principles of life, faith, and relationships that will help you focus on your overall health and well-being this first semester in college.

I remember being in my youth group in high school and learning that I should have a daily quiet time. I would come home from a weekend camp and get fired up about having a quiet time. Even though I was not a morning person, I would plan to get up even earlier and read a devotional book before getting ready for school. And that is exactly what I did…for about two days. On day three I forgot and overslept; then I felt like it was wasted. I had failed, so I just stopped. Another season would go by, and I would get fired up again, only to forget a few days into my newest commitment. As I got older, I began to see that the traditional devotional format was not what I needed. Growing in your faith does not happen simply by reading two paragraphs, one verse, and a three sentence prayer. It is learning and understanding what it means to apply your faith to the world around you and learning how to live out the words of Scripture.

Regardless of how your high school "quiet time" might have gone, I am going to offer you a new method of spending time in Scripture and in prayer.

The structure of this devotional book is set up to 1) help you apply the principles of the Christian faith to the life of a college student and 2) help you develop a pattern of spending time with God in reflection and prayer, as you are challenged and encouraged.

In this book you will spend a full week on one of the 15 principles of faith. On day one you will read a traditional devotional, and on another day you will read a narrative about that same topic. Then around midweek you will answer some questions related to your reading, and finally you will exercise your faith through a challenge.

Here is what that will look like.

Monday: Read a short introductory message on this week's faith principle. This should only take you a few minutes. You will also be given a verse that you will be challenged to memorize that week.

Tuesday: Read a short story that will help you understand this life principle in the setting of college. As a freshman, you will be experiencing new things every day. Tuesday's reading will give you a glimpse into faith and college life.

Wednesday: Answer a few questions about the week's message and how it is encouraging you to grow in your relationship with Christ in college. These questions can be answered in the book, in another notebook, &/or shared with a friend for accountability. You will also be encouraged to continue learning the Scripture of the Week so that you can quote it from memory by the weekend.

Thursday: In college, Thursday is often considered the last day of the work week. On Thursday, you will be given a challenge for the weekend to exercise your faith and put this principle into practice.

Friday/Weekend: Review all that has been said this week through the book and in your answers to the questions. Focus on the Weekly Challenge and spend the weekend living out your faith to those around you.

This book is designed for a freshman during the first semester of college. If you are picking up this book at another time, don't put it down. These faith principles are relevant in any stage of life. The writings and questions will be speaking to a first semester college student, but wherever you are in your journey of life and faith, you can gain wisdom from these pages.

Know who you are and

WEEK ONE

why that's important.

Therefore, if anyone is in Christ, he is a new creation. The old has passed away; behold, the new has come. 2 Corinthians 5:17

Monday

On your first day of college, no one knows your name. Unlike high school where many knew you, college is a fresh start. For some people, this is exciting and for others it is pretty scary. Regardless, before other people can truly know you, you must be sure that you know yourself.

The world is filled with answers to the question: "Who am I?" It is important to answer that question for yourself before other voices in the world, and on campus, try to tell you who they want you to be. Our identity stems from our foundation, the solid ground on which we stand. If your foundation is based on your appearance, then you will be consumed with being someone who looks the part. If your identity is in your ability, your talents, or your intelligence, then you will feel lost when you fail and are unable to live up to your own expectations.

In 2 Corinthians 5:17, Paul tells us that, as Christians, our identity should be found in our relationship with Jesus and nothing else. He assures us that those failed attempts to identify ourselves in any other way is as old as high school. Your former identity, the person you used to be, has now passed away and you are a new creation in Jesus.

This good news is good timing for you because you are starting a fresh chapter in your life that is as new as your identity in Christ. The people you are meeting in college will only know the person they meet and see in you. Let that be someone who stands on the foundation of his relationship with Jesus. You are a new creation, and this is Day One.

Now, spend a couple minutes in prayer as you talk to God about who you are in Christ. Ask God to give you the confidence to be who He has made you to be, and to lead you to others who you can have community with in Christ. Pray that you will be surrounded with opportunities to find new friends who will help you grow in your faith. Ask God to transform you to be more like Jesus little by little, day by day.

Tuesday

Sam was sitting in class on his first day of college. A mixture of nervous excitement spun circles in his stomach as he realized his class was filled with perfect strangers. He recognized some faces from his dorm and from orientation, but he wasn't sure if anyone remembered his name. In high school, Sam had a lot of friends. He wasn't the most popular guy in school, but he was well liked by enough people to feel good about it most of the time. As he looked around, he felt like the only one who was nervous and insecure about starting over to make new friends. As he turned around to the row behind him, two other freshman looked at him and said hello. Chase and Nora had met while walking to class and were sitting behind Sam. They invited Sam to lunch after class, and he accepted. This will be the first real opportunity for Sam to meet some new friends in college, and now he has a decision to make. Will he be himself and trust that they will like him for who he is? Will he stand on the foundation of who he is in Christ, even if they are not believers themselves? Will he trust God's leading in his life to answer his prayer for community and friends in the faith? What would you do if you were in Sam's situation?

Fill in the blank as you learn this verse this week:

Therefore, if anyone is in Christ, he is a _____ creation. The _____ has passed away; behold, the new has come. 2 Corinthians 5:17

Spend some time in prayer and ask for confidence in who you are and how you want others to see you. Get out your Bible and read 2 Corinthians 5:17-21 and see who you are and why you are a new creation.

Wednesday

Fill in the blank:

Therefore, if _____ is in _____, he is a _____
creation. The _____ has passed away; behold, the
new has _____. 2 Corinthians ___:17

Spend some time thinking through your answers to
these questions. Write your answers in the space
provided or in another notebook/journal.

Describe how you think others saw you in high school.
What characteristics would they use to describe the
high-school-you?

Looking back at the description you just listed, how well did your friends really know you in high school?

What characteristics about yourself do you want to change as you make new friends in college?

Do your answers to the last question reflect a foundation of faith in Jesus or one of the world? In other words, do you want others to see your Christ-like kindness and compassion, or do you hope they think you are the most attractive and talented person in the room? Spend some time evaluating your heart and who you are in Christ because any other identity perception is fooling yourself and everyone who knows you.

Thursday

Every Thursday you will be given a challenge based on the topic of the week. This week's challenge is to determine how you are to act based on who you are in Christ. Below are some identity-based verses. Spend some time over the next few days to look them up, copy them down, and then write a description of how it helps you stand on the foundation of who you are in Christ.

Example:
1 Corinthians 12:27: Now you are the body of Christ, and each one of you is a part of it.
This means: That I need to find a church to be a part of and be involved in it.

John 1:12:

This means:

1 Corinthians 6:19-20:

This means:

Ephesians 2:10:

This means:

Ephesians 3:12:

This means:

Matthew 5:14-15

This means:

I John 4:4

This means:

Weekend Review

Spend time this weekend reviewing this week's lesson and your answers to the questions.

Optional weekend reading: Mark 1

WEEK ONE NOTES:

Know why community matters
WEEK TWO
and how to build it

And day by day, attending the temple together and breaking bread in their homes, they received their food with glad and generous hearts, praising God and having favor with all the people. Acts 2:46-47

Monday

College is a very social place. As you have probably already noticed, the social world of college is different than high school. First of all, everyone is older; and therefore, college relationships are often more mature than before. For those who live on campus, college friends include roommates and people who see each other at all hours of the day and night. Typically, you know your college friends deeper for all of these reasons. Because of that, it has never been more important to understand the value of community and how to build it.

There is a difference in having friends and having community. You will know a lot of people in college. You will have friends in class, people who live down the hall in the dorm, and friends you see around campus. You might spend a lot of time with them but never develop community with them. Community is a deeper level of relationship: one that is based on a common foundation. Last week we talked about identity and how who you are is drawn from the foundation that you stand on. When you find other people who share the same foundational identity, you can have community.

In Acts 2:46-47, the Christians in the early church understood community. They lived together, ate together, learned together, and hung out all the time....sound familiar? In Acts we see some important components to developing community. First, you grow in Christ together. It says that on a regular basis, these friends went to the temple (Jewish church). They would have worshiped and learned God's Word together. That was the foundation of their relationship and will be what makes your community solid and healthy. Secondly. they ate together. Eating is one of the most intimate things we do with our friends. It is a time to talk, laugh, and share life together. Third, the passage says that they had favor with all people, meaning that they were generous, inclusive, and gracious with others. We also know from the verses before and after this passage that they served together in ministry.

In college, you will have a lot of opportunities to be in groups of friends. You might join social organizations, service clubs, and campus ministry groups. These groups may or may not become true community. In all of your social activities, be sure to seek out a group of friends who you can spend quality time with, grow together in Christ, keep one another accountable, and make an impact together on those around you. Then you will find community.

Spend some time in prayer about finding Christ-centered community on campus.

Tuesday

Chase has met a lot of people in his first couple of weeks of college, and out of all of these new college friends, his closest friends are Sam, Nora, JT, and Emma. JT and Chase are roommates, and the others all met in class during the first week. Nora and Sam went through rush and are now pretty busy in their respective new pledge classes. Emma is running for SGA, and Chase is thinking about asking Nora out on a date. Each person is seeking friendships outside of the group, but there is one thing that all five friends have in common: they are all going together each week to a campus ministry worship gathering and building community based on a mutual faith in Jesus. Before long, Chase, JT, Sam, Nora, and Emma are eating together regularly, talking about their faith with one another, and thinking about all going on a weekend retreat hosted by a church in town. It isn't that they spend all of their time together, but they know that they need each other, and they need this community. One thing they have all realized is that they have been called to love God and love others, and that there is no better way to follow Jesus than to follow Him with others in community. No other group provides the level of accountability, trust, dedication, and devotion than what these friends have found with each other. This is so important to each of them and is worth protecting and nurturing.

Fill in the blank as you learn this verse this week:

And day by day, attending the temple _____ and breaking bread in their _____, they received their food with glad and generous hearts, praising God and having _____ with all the people. Acts 2:46-47

Spend a few minutes in prayer and ask God to show you opportunities to develop community with others on campus. Get out your Bible and read Acts 2:42-47 to learn more about the first century Christians in community.

Wednesday

Fill in the blank:

And _____ by day, attending the _____ _____ and breaking _____ in their _____, they received their food with glad and generous _____, _____ God and having _____ with all the people. Acts __:46-47

List some adjectives that come to mind when you read the entire passage of Acts 2:42-47.

Describe a community that you had in high school at school or at church.

What would be the benefits of developing Christ-centered community during your freshman year? What would be the benefits of remaining in a group like that three or four years from now?

Who are some people you have met or seen on campus that you would enjoy developing this level of friendship with?

Thursday

Just like last week, it is time to put this principle into practice and develop a vision for what you are seeking in community. This assignment is a three-step process. First you will set a goal, then make a plan, and third you will execute the plan.

Set A Goal For Community:

Who do you already know that would be interested in developing a Christ-centered community? (See your list from question four from yesterday.)

Where should you look for like-hearted students? (Think about campus ministries and churches with active college ministries.)

What is an activity that you could casually pull together to include some of these friends?

Make A Plan:

Develop a plan to get some of these friends together and decide what you will discuss. Depending on how well you know them, you might start out by pulling together some Christian friends and see if anything develops from it. If you are already close, consider asking them to start a Bible Study or prayer group to see how interested they are in growing spiritually in accountability with other Christian friends.

Execute The Plan:

Be the leader and make it happen. Otherwise, this type of friendship might never develop. Your community doesn't have to be a small group of 5 people. It might start from a larger group from a church, but the closer you are the more everyone will benefit from community.

Weekend Review

Spend time this weekend reviewing this week's lesson and your answers to the questions.

Optional weekend reading: Mark 2

WEEK TWO NOTES:

Know why you need a church

WEEK THREE

and how to find one

And let us consider how to stir up one another to love and good works, not neglecting to meet together, as is the habit of some, but encouraging one another, and all the more as you see the Day drawing near.
Hebrews 10:24-25

Monday

As this verse suggests, "some" are in the habit of neglecting to meet together with other believers. For whatever reason, they are not involved in the community of the church and therefore miss out on the encouragement in the faith that every Christian needs. In college, this is often the majority, rather than the minority. For some, it is due to a transition overload in a new environment that requires a student to adjust to so many new things at once. For others, it is a form of laziness or irresponsibility in trying to avoid making as many responsible decisions as possible. Whatever the reason, you should know the importance of finding a church as soon as possible in college so that you can thrive in every other part of your life.

Joining a local church will give you many opportunities that no other body will (not even a campus ministry), because the church is unlike anything else. First of all, the Church is the bride of Christ (Ephesians 5:22). Church was God's idea, and it is filled with His people. The church will allow you to participate in the Gospel. Jesus said to go, tell, baptize, and disciple (Matt 28), and this is the calling of the church. Through serving together, loving others, and sharing your faith with people, you are fulfilling the commission of ministry. The church will also help you discover and exercise your gifts. As we learn in 1 Corinthians 12, we all have different spiritual gifts which are to be used to lead, encourage, and serve people in Christ. When we do this alongside other believers, we form the full body of Christ. Lastly, the church will provide you with spiritual leadership and authority through mentors and other adults. God will put these people in your life to teach you and help you grow. As Hebrews 13:17 says, "Have confidence in your leaders and submit to their authority, because they keep watch over you as those who must give an account."

The core of all people is the soul. The soul is the spiritual part of you. This is the center of your life because you were created by God. For those who believe in God, this makes sense as you work to remain healthy in your spirit. When our soul is healthy, every other aspect of our life will be healthy as well. This includes our relationships, our thoughts, our decisions, and our physical and emotional health. Therefore, the simplest answer to the question, "Why do you need to be involved in a church?" is because the church will make your soul healthy and help you be and do all that you were created for.

Spend some time in prayer and ask God to reveal to you the importance of His Church in your life and in the lives of those around you.

Tuesday

JT grew up in a family that was always at church. His father was the pastor, and he was there all the time. By the time he got to his junior year in high school, JT was tired of church. His youth group seemed to do the same things every year, and he became bored with it. He told himself that when he got to college, he would do what he wanted to do which probably meant not going to church every week. After he moved into his dorm room, he met Chase. Chase had a different church experience in high school. Chase did not grow up in a church as a kid but was invited to a camp the summer after 10th grade. That week at camp, he met Jesus and jumped head first into the youth group. He loved the worship events, mission trips, and learning about all the stories in the Bible that everyone else seemed to grow up hearing. The first day Chase met JT, he asked him about going to church. JT was surprised that his new roommate was so excited about something that he felt was boring and dull. That night JT laid in bed and thought about why he didn't want to find a church. He realized that the problem was more in his heart than it was with church. He wasn't sure if he would go with Chase on Sunday, but he felt like he probably should give it another chance.

Fill in the blank as you learn this verse this week:

And let us consider how to stir up one _____ to love and _____ _____, not neglecting to meet _____, as is the habit of some, but _____ one another, and all the more as you see the Day drawing near. Hebrews 10:24-25

Spend a few minutes in prayer and then read Hebrews 10:19-25 and look for examples of church in this passage.

Wednesday

Fill in the blank

And let us _____ how to stir up one another to
_____ and good works, not _____ to meet
together, as is the _____ of some, but
_____ one another, and all the more as you see
the Day drawing near. Hebrews ___:24-25

How would you describe your experience with church
in high school? What did you like about it, and what
did you dislike? What did you learn from it, and what
parts of it will you miss?

Make a list of all the benefits of the local church. These are not just benefits for you, but in general, what good does the church do in the community and beyond?

What are you looking for in a local church at this stage of your life in college?

Make a list of five churches in the area that you would consider visiting. Make sure that all of these churches are consistent with the Bible and are centered on the Gospel. If you are unsure, look online and/or talk to some older college students.

Thursday

This week's challenge is called "Find a Church By Thanksgiving" and is adapted from page 228 of my book *Lost in Transition: Becoming Spiritually Prepared For College.*

Step One: Find five churches you want to visit in the area. Hopefully you made your list yesterday in the last question. Also, find a friend or two who want to join in on the fun.

Step Two: This Sunday, go visit the first church on your list. In my book I suggest you do this on the first Sunday of September. It doesn't matter if that is when you start, just start this Sunday. Next Sunday, go and visit the second church on your list until you have visited all five.

Step Three: After visiting all five churches on your list, pick your top three and drop the bottom two. Now go back and re-visit those three churches.

Step Four: You are now going to pick your favorite two churches and drop the other one. Go and visit those two churches again. This should be the third time you have gone to these churches. Take some time to learn as much about them as you can.

Step Five: Pick the church that you like the best out of the two. This church should be the one where you feel most at home and are more likely to want to attend consistently. Next Sunday, go back and join that church.

Step Six: Tell your parents that you have found a church during your first semester in college. By doing this, you are way ahead of the curve, and you can now get involved and allow this church body to build you up as you join them in changing the world.

Weekend Review

Spend time this weekend reviewing this week's lesson and your answers to the questions.

Optional weekend reading: Mark 3

WEEK THREE NOTES:

Know what makes a good friend
WEEK FOUR
and how to be one

Walk with the wise and become wise, for a companion of fools suffers harm. Proverbs 13:20

Monday

What makes a good friend? Think about that for a moment. If you have had a good, dependable friend in your life, think about why they were your friend. This is important to understand the qualities of a good friend so that you know what you are looking for.

The Bible is filled with good advice for finding friends. The general theme is that you need to make sure that your closest friends are of good character because they will influence you. Proverbs 13:20 is the chief of these verses as it instructs you to find wise friends so that you too will become wise, for foolishness is contagious as well. In the Bible, foolishness is the opposite of wisdom, and wisdom is a perspective of seeing the world as God sees it. If you want to pursue wisdom and truth in your life, you need to insure that your closest friends do as well. As 1 Corinthians 15:33 says: "Bad company corrupts good character."

College is a very social place. Your friendships in college will potentially be deeper than any group of friends you have ever had. Statistics also tell us that the friends you make in college will most likely be lifelong relationships. That is another important reason to choose your friends wisely and take the time to invest in those relationships.

According to Scripture, you want to find a friend who is dependable, someone who will offer you accountability, and one who will value you over themselves.

Dependability: Proverbs 18:24 says, "One who has unreliable friends soon comes to ruin, but there is a friend who sticks closer than a brother." If you can not trust a friend, you do not have a solid foundation to build a friendship. This verse suggests that a good friend is someone that you can trust as much as you should trust a brother. Trust develops over time which is why your closest friends need to be as dedicated to following Jesus as you are.

Accountability: Accountability is a mutual decision, between you and a friend, to help one another stay healthy in your life and faith. As Proverbs 27:17 so famously explains: "As iron sharpens iron, so one person sharpens another." In the same way that iron is sharpened by striking it with another piece of iron, friends need to make each other sharper through the bond of accountability. If you can not have this level of friendship with someone, they might not be the right person to be one of your closest friends.

Selflessness: Commonly known as the Golden Rule, Luke 6:31 says,"Do to others as you would have them do to you." This is a selfless love for a friend that puts someone else's needs over her own. Jesus modeled this in John 15:12-15 when He said, "My command is this: Love each other as I have loved you. Greater love has no one than this: to lay down one's life for one's friends. You are my friends if you do what I command. I no longer call you servants, because a servant does not know his master's business. Instead, I have called you friends, for everything that I learned from my Father I have made known to you."

This is the type of person you want as a friend, and the best way to attract this person is to be this type of friend as well. Be a dependable friend who offers accountability and loves selflessly. Then you will draw people to you who will be sharpened by your strength and made wise through your wisdom.

Tuesday

Sam, Nora, Emma. JT and Chase have been friends for a few weeks now and have really gotten to know each other pretty well. They get along, have similar interests, and respect one another. They are all in a small group together that was started by a church on campus and have begun to grow and encourage each other in their walk with Christ. The other day they all volunteered to work a booth for their church at an organization fair on the quad, but Sam did not show up for his scheduled time. This was not the first time that Sam had let the group down. He had missed a few other things and was beginning to show himself to be undependable. Nora, Emma. JT and Chase talked about what they could do. JT and Emma didn't want to bring it up to Sam, but Nora and Chase knew they needed to. They felt that if their friendship was going to be based on trust, then accountability needed to be a key condition. They all approached Sam, and in a loving way, helped him to see how important it is that he be dependable as a friend by doing what he says he is going to do.

Fill in the blank as you learn this verse this week:

Walk with the _____ and become _____,
for a companion of _____ suffers
_____. Proverbs 13:20

Spend a few minutes in prayer and then read Proverbs 18:24, 27:17 and John 15:12-15 again.

Wednesday

Fill in the blank

_____ with the _____ and become
_____, for a _____ of _____
suffers _____. Proverbs ___:20

After looking at all the verses listed this week about
friendship, list as many qualities and characteristics
that you can for how the Bible describes a good friend.

After reading Tuesday's story about Sam and his
friends, write out what you would do if you were Sam
(you had missed your commitment) and what you
would do if you were the friends (you had a friend
who let you down).

Make a list of your new college friends and list a positive character quality about each one. (Here are some character qualities you might choose from: kind, friendly, generous, forgiving, fun, cheerful, understanding, considerate, wise, dependable, selfless, loving, patient).

When it comes to finding a good friend, it takes one to know one. List three things that you can do to be a more dependable, considerate friend to others.

Thursday

The challenge for this week is to help you become a better friend to those around you. Galatians 5:22-23 is what we call The Fruit of the Spirit. This is a list of 9 qualities of someone who is a follower of Jesus. These "fruits" grow out of the overflow of your heart in Christ and provide evidence to others about your faith. The best way to be a good friend is to live out these 9 characteristics in everything you do.

Below, list a task that you can do that represents each of the The Fruit of the Spirit.

Love:

Joy:

Peace:

Patience:

Kindness:

Goodness:

Faithfulness:

Gentleness:

Self-control:

Weekend Review

Spend time this weekend reviewing this week's lesson and your answers to the questions.

Optional weekend reading: Mark 4

WEEK FOUR NOTES:

Know what you believe
WEEK FIVE
and how to express it

"Always be prepared to give an answer to everyone who asks you to give a reason for the hope that you have." 1 Peter 3:15

Monday

In college, you will be tested in what you believe. Now, stop and read that sentence again because it is true. One of the number one reasons that a Christian stops believing in Jesus is because that person did not totally understand what they claimed to believe before they were challenged in their faith. The Bible is filled with warnings about knowing what you believe so that you can explain it. In 1 Peter 3:15, you are instructed to be prepared to answer someone that asks you what you believe. This is important for three reasons.

First, it is important because the person asking needs the Gospel as much as you. The last thing Jesus told his followers before ascending to Heaven is found in Matthew 28:19-20: "Therefore go and make disciples of all nations, baptizing them in the name of the Father and of the Son and of the Holy Spirit, and teaching them to obey everything I have commanded you." We are instructed to tell others, so they can believe. Secondly, we need to be prepared to answer for our faith because Christianity is true. If you believe in Jesus, you believe the truth. Jesus Himself said this in John 14:6 when He describes himself as "The Truth." To believe in truth and to keep that to yourself is the very opposite of loving others. Thirdly, you need to know what you believe and how to express it because those who might challenge you will know what they believe and how they will express it. The sure way to make a truth seem false is to waver and not give a confident explanation.

So how can you become prepared to give an answer to those who ask you about what you believe? The first thing you do is to know what you believe by reading Scripture and learning what the Bible says. The Bible is our guide. According to 2 Timothy 3:16, Scripture is useful for "teaching, rebuking, correcting and training in righteousness." Let the Bible teach you truth and train you in expressing what you believe, so that you can rebuke falsehoods and correct those who speak against God's Word. After you begin to learn what you believe, create an outline of your worldview based on your understanding of Scripture. You might consider talking to a mentor to help you fill in any gaps you might be missing. Then, practice explaining it so that your rebuttal comes naturally out of your mouth. Find a friend and have a mock debate. Discuss this with other Christian friends in hopes of training yourself in apologetics (the word apologetics comes from 1 Peter 3:15 and means to give an answer or a defense for your reason or belief.)

Tuesday

Nora was excited about her introduction to Philosophy class because she loved to have discussions about various beliefs and understandings. She had heard stories about the professor and how he treated Christians in his classes but felt that she would be able to learn from the open forum in class. On the first day, Dr. Matthews introduced himself, welcomed everyone to Philosophy 101, and explained the first assignment that was due at the beginning of the next class. The assignment was for each student to state the religious belief they were raised on and then give an argument for why it is not true. The professor added that the argument must be thorough and believable. Nora left the class in tears as she did not understand how she could disprove her faith in Jesus. That night she talked to Chase and Emma about the assignment. Chase suggested that she not do it. He said that she should take a stand and refuse to write on such a ridiculous topic. Emma had a different suggestion. Emma said that Nora should do the paper and let it serve as an opportunity to strengthen her beliefs and worldview. Explaining this point, Emma added that by taking the antagonistic approach, she will better understand what she believes and how to construct a defense against the argument.

Fill in the blank as you learn this verse this week:

"_____ be prepared to give an _____ to everyone who asks you to give a _____ for the _____ that you have." 1 Peter 3:15

Spend a few minutes in prayer before going on with the rest of your week.

Wednesday

Fill in the blank

_____ be _____ to give an
_____ to everyone who _____ _____ to
give a _____ for the _____ that you
have." 1 Peter 3:____

Write out a personal statement of faith based on what
you believe and know to be true.

List as many Bible verses to support the statement of
faith you just wrote.

What are some of the common arguments against your statement of faith that non-believers might have?

Why do you think atheist/agnostics disbelieve Christianity?

Thursday

This week's challenge is to have a mock debate with a fellow Christian. This is an opportunity for you both to develop your understanding of what you believe as Christians. Here are a few guidelines.

1. Be sure that you do this with someone who believes what you believe. It is important that this does not turn into a real debate, which might confuse both of you.
2. Prepare your answers beforehand so that you are not simply talking off the top of your head.
3. Make sure that no one raises their voice or gets angry, even in the spirit of acting. If you were in an actual conversation with a non-believer, you would want to stay calm and deliver your point in a peaceful manner.

For your discussion, use these questions on the next page to structure your debate. Plan to have two rounds, so that each of you can be the Christian and the non-Christian. For each question, the person playing the non-Christian will ask the question to the Christian and then challenge the answer with another question.

Question 1: How is Christianity different from other religions?

Question 2: What proof do you have for what you believe about Jesus?

Question 3: Why do Christians seem to be against more things than they are for?

As you prepare for these questions, here are some ideas for structuring your answer.

Question one deals with how Christianity compares with other religions. The main difference in every other religion is found in the person of Jesus. No other belief system is centered around a person who claimed to be God, died for the sins of the world, and then came back to life. Every other religion is based on proving one's worth to a higher being in hopes of pleasing him, whereas Christianity is built upon the grace of salvation at the cross.

Question two is based on the person of Jesus. The worldly approach to belief is based on proof, yet no one can prove that God does not exist. Scripture even talks about nature being a proof that God exists. The best "proof" for Jesus is based on eye witnesses to what He said and did. Start there to answer this question.

Question three focuses on how Christian's view and treat other people. Non-believers feel that Christians hate non-Christians because we don't accept their non-Biblical behavior. First, no one should judge Christianity by looking at Christians, because all Christians are sinners. Rather, Christianity should be understood by looking at the words and actions of Jesus. To understand how Christians view other people, one needs to look at how Jesus related to non-believers.

Weekend Review

Spend time this weekend reviewing this week's lesson and your answers to the questions.

Optional weekend reading: Mark 5

WEEK FIVE NOTES:

Know what wisdom is

WEEK SIX

and how to use it

The fear of the Lord is the beginning of wisdom; all those who practice it have a good understanding.
Psalm 111:10

Monday

Many people define the words "wisdom" and "knowledge" as the same thing, but they have very different meanings in Scripture. Knowledge is typically something you learn in a book, like algebra or history. Wisdom is an understanding of right and wrong and comes with knowing God. In Psalm 111:10, we see that the beginning of wisdom comes from a fear of the Lord (this "fear" is not being afraid of God but rather, respecting His power and obeying His Word). This passage then tells us that those who practice wisdom will gain a Godly understanding.

The Bible talks a lot about wisdom, and yet it is not very common in our world today. The reason for this is because Godly wisdom and worldly knowledge are often at odds with one another. One example of this is found in Proverbs 3:5: "Trust in the Lord with all your heart, and do not lean on your own understanding." Worldly knowledge is based solely on what can be explained and understood by the human mind. Even though there are a lot of smart people in the world, we live in a world that lacks wisdom.

So, how do you get wisdom? James 1:5 clearly answers that question by saying, "If any of you lacks wisdom, let him ask God, who gives generously to all without reproach, and it will be given him." Another step in gaining wisdom is to immerse yourself in God's Word. Colossians 3:16 says, "Let the word of Christ dwell in you richly, teaching and admonishing one another in all wisdom, singing psalms and hymns and spiritual songs, with thankfulness in your hearts to God."

How do you know that you have gained wisdom? Like other attributes of following Jesus, wisdom will be revealed in the fruit of your actions. As James 3:13 says, "Who is wise and understanding among you? By his good conduct let him show his works in the meekness of wisdom." You know you have wisdom when you begin making wise choices. You will know that your decisions are filled with wisdom when they are consistent with God's Word.

So, how is gaining wisdom related to your first year in college? You now have more freedom than you may have ever had in your life. You are in a position to make more decisions on your own than ever before. Also, those decisions will have a bigger effect on your life than in your past. This means that one right decision could lead you into a life-long opportunity, but it also means that one poor decision could have major, life-altering consequences. Using wisdom - praying, reading Scripture, seeking counsel - is necessary to your development as a young adult and will prepare you for your life better than anything else you could do.

Tuesday

In high school, JT was the guy everyone looked up to. He was the one who seemed to always do everything right. This wasn't always true, but the image he had developed was that of the good Christian. When he got to college, he wanted to be free from that stigma and have a lifestyle that seemed more relaxed from the rules of his faith. Within the first few weeks of college, JT had gotten to know a group of guys on the second floor of the dorm. These guys are what JT would have called the "party crowd" in high school, but they just seemed to have fun and live care-free. JT first met these guys one night after hearing the theme music to one of his favorite video games playing in the distance. Soon, he was hanging out and playing video games every night with his new friends from the second floor until around 4:00 am the next morning. Soon, he began missing his early classes because of his new late night routine. After a few times, Chase began to notice a change in JT, and so he asked him about it. JT blew it off, but Chase challenged him to think about how his decisions were affecting him. In just a few weeks' time, JT had gone from a responsible, level-headed roommate making good grades and growing spiritually, to a guy who was missing class, failing history, drinking beer, and smoking pot, all because of some recent unwise decisions. After thinking about it, JT began to see the difference in his life. He realized that he needed to decide which path he really wanted to take, and which life better matched the person he truly wanted to be.

Fill in the blank as you learn this verse this week:

The _____ of the Lord is the beginning of _____; all those who practice it have a good _____. Psalm 111:10

Spend a few minutes in prayer asking God to give you wisdom and lead you to friends who are making wise decisions as well.

Wednesday

Fill in the blank

The _____ of the _____ is the _____ of
_____; all those who _____ it have a good
_____. Psalm _____:_____

In your own words, what is wisdom and why is it
important?

How have you seen someone (or maybe yourself) use
wisdom to make an important decision?

What are some other factors, other than wisdom, that someone might use to make a decision?

List at least five scenarios in college in which using wisdom would be helpful in making the right decision.

Thursday

For your challenge this week, look up the following ten verses about wisdom and give a one sentence explanation for how you can use that advice during your time in college.

Proverbs 1:7

Proverbs 4:6-7

1 Corinthians 1:25

Proverbs 19:20

Proverbs 3:13-18

Proverbs 11:2

Proverbs 16:16

Matthew 7:24

Ephesians 5:15-16

Colossians 4:5-6

Weekend Review

Spend time this weekend reviewing this week's lesson and your answers to the questions.

Optional weekend reading: Mark 6

WEEK SIX NOTES:

Know what you want out of life
WEEK SEVEN
and how to get it

Where there is no vision, the people perish.
Proverbs 29:18

Monday

Baseball legend, Yogi Berra, is famous for many funny sayings, like "Ninety percent of the game is half mental" and "it's like deja vu all over again", but one of the truest Yogi Berra sayings is this: "If you don't know where you are going, you'll end up someplace else." It is always important to know where you are going in your life so that you can focus on what it takes to get there. Proverbs 29:18 is a great reminder that when we do not have a plan and a direction for our lives, we end up wandering around wasting our time.

Like never before in your life, your time in college will serve as a marker for what you want to do and get out of life. One day, when you are older, you will look back on the decisions you made in college and how they have impacted your life. For some, the decisions will seem to form a path that is straight and direct, but for others, the journey might reflect a series of unnecessary detours.

Every decision from picking a major to joining social groups will affect the rest of your life. This is why it is important to be intentional about making these decisions, while seeking counsel and using wisdom.

Here are three things to consider as you think about what you want to get out of life and how you will go about getting it. First, seek the Lord for guidance. God already knows the path of your life, and He has great plans in mind for you (see Jeremiah 29:11). But one thing you must understand is that God's plans are not always the same as your plans. As Proverbs 16:3 tells us: "Many are the plans in the mind of a man, but it is the purpose of the Lord that will stand."

Secondly, trust the Lord that He will lead you down the path of life that is the most suited for you. As Proverbs 16:3 says, "Commit your work to the Lord, and your plans will be established." So many times people focus on what they want out of life without asking God what He wants for them. Something that I have always believed is that the Lord has given you all the gifts, talents, relationships, and opportunities you will need to live your life to the fullest, and it is up to you to find that path and walk in it.

The third thing is to allow others to advise and direct you. Often we can only see our life through the narrowest of perspectives, and we need someone else to speak truth in our life. One thing to be careful about is to make sure that the voices you are listening to are seeking God's direction on your behalf. The Lord will give you a better life than you could ever give yourself, but you have to identify it and pursue that life with all your heart.

Tuesday

Emma had always thought that she would be an attorney when she grew up. Her mother practiced law, and her brother was in his second year of law school. Growing up, she was always told that she would make a good lawyer because she was very convincing and good at debate. Then, during her senior year in high school, she got very close to her English literature teacher and began to think about becoming a teacher. The summer before starting college, Emma took a career assessment test which also concluded that she would be good at teaching older students. When it came time to declare a major for college, Emma committed to pre-law because that was what she was always told. With the idea of teaching growing stronger in her heart, Emma began to doubt her direction in life. Should she change her major before it is too late? Who should she talk to about her options? What she should do? These are all the questions rushing around Emma's mind as she thought about the life she was called to live.

Fill in the blank as you learn this verse this week:

Where there is no _____, the _____
_____. Proverbs _____:18

Spend a few minutes in prayer about your future and the steps you should take to determine God's direction for your life.

Wednesday

Fill in the blank of this entire verse

_____ _____ is _____
_____, the _____ _____.
Proverbs ____:_____

What have you always thought you would do for a living? List three reasons why you think you should or should not still pursue that career field.

Why do you think it is important to know God's plans for your life before you set out on your own ideas?

What other life plans do you have, other than career, that you need to dedicate to the Lord?

Who are some mentors and advisers in your life that can help you determine what you want out of life and how to get it?

Thursday

This week's challenge is to create some goals for yourself. For some people, this is easier than for others. Below is a guide to use as you create a plan for yourself academically, socially, spiritually, and personally.

Academic goals are ones that lead you to a major and a career. Social goals will include groups to be a part of and long-term friend goals. Spiritual goals will include your church involvement, levels of maturity and growth, and even ministry opportunities to participate in. Personal goals might be physical goals (lose weight, work out, get more sleep), time management related, or a desire to develop a skill or talent. Think of one goal in each of the four categories and take that idea through these three steps.

The first step in goal setting is understanding what it is that we want to accomplish. This will include spending time in prayer in search of God's direction and plan.

The second step is to create realistic, viable goals. Goals need to be specific, clear, and attainable. This means that they need to be measurable and include a starting and ending point. The truth is, a goal without specifics is just a dream.

The third step in the process is to develop actionable steps to accomplish the goal. You may need to identity the obstacles that are in your way and lay out the necessary "mini-goals" that need to be reached in order to get closer to the main goal.

Weekend Review

Spend time this weekend reviewing this week's lesson and your answers to the questions.

Optional weekend reading: Mark 7

WEEK SEVEN NOTES:

Know the importance of a good
WEEK EIGHT
character and how to develop it

Whoever walks in integrity walks securely, but he who
makes his ways crooked will be found out.
Proverbs 10:9

Monday

There are few things more important than having a good character, but what is character? Character is who you are, at your core, and how that makes you act. Character is more than a reputation, because a reputation is what others know about how you act. Character is often identified more in how you act when no one is watching rather than when you are on display. Integrity is what fuels good character. Integrity is the act of being honest and true to your good character. In Proverbs 10:9, we see that those who walk in integrity will live securely, but those who lack integrity will be discovered as such.

What does it mean when it says that those with integrity will live securely? Think about it this way. If you don't break the law, then when you pass a police car on the road, you should not worry because the officer has no reason to pull you over. You are secure because you are in good standing with the law. The same could be said about character. If you are always honest and truthful, you have no reason to worry about someone catching you in a lie.

The first step in developing a good character is to be sure your mind is focused on purity and truth. As Jesus said in Matthew 12:34: "For the mouth speaks what the heart is full of." You can't fake integrity, at least not for long. Romans 12:2 tells us not to allow the world to mold us, but rather to be transformed by renewing our minds in Christ. This renewal of your mind is the first step to developing integrity and a good character.

Philippians 4:8 is an important verse for developing a good character because it is very specific in what you should be thinking about. It says: "Whatever is true, whatever is honorable, whatever is just, whatever is pure, whatever is lovely, whatever is commendable, if there is any excellence, if there is anything worthy of praise, think about these things." This is not easy, especially if you are living in a typical college environment where the behavior of those around you are not focused on these things. This is why, as we have already studied in this book, it is critical to surround yourself with others who are focused on Jesus and walking daily with Him.

After you focus your mind on purity, love, truth, and all things Jesus, you need to allow the fruit of the Spirit to flow through you. The fruit of the Spirit, found in Galatians 5:22-23, are qualities of someone with a good character. You may be familiar with this passage already, but let's look at it again. "But the fruit of the Spirit is love, joy, peace, patience, kindness, goodness, faithfulness, gentleness, self-control; against such things there is no law." Focus on truth and purity and live out love, peace, kindness, and self-control, and you will naturally be of good character. Then you will love "securely" without fear of loosing the trust of others around you.

Tuesday

It was about 2:00am when Sam discovered that he had a major chemistry test the next morning. He had not kept up with his syllabus as well as he should have, and now he was not sure what to do. He was already tired and estimated that it would take him at least three hours to review his notes and prepare for the test. He could barely stay awake as he began reading about elements, compounds, and mixtures. When Sam's roommate Collin realized that Sam had not studied, he offered to give him the answers since Collin was taking the same test an hour before. Collin offered to take a picture with his phone of his paper before he turned it in so that Sam could copy it. Knowing that Collin knew the material and that it would be hard for the professor to catch them since they were in different classes, Sam was strongly considering it. He knew that he would fail the test if he didn't have Collin's answers, but he also knew in his heart that this was wrong. He accepted Collin's offer that night but was still unsure if he could go through with the act once it was time to take the test. What if he got caught? What if it worked out, but he felt guilty afterwards? These were important questions that were consuming him as he lay in bed that night.

Fill in the blank as you learn this verse this week:

Whoever walks in _____ walks _____, but he who makes his ways _____ will be found out. Proverbs ____:9

Spend some time in prayer asking God to give you a clean heart: one that is focused on purity and truth.

Wednesday

Fill in the blank of this entire verse

Whoever _____ in _____ walks _____ , but he who makes his _____ _____ will be _____ _____. _____ ___:_____

Who do you know that is a great example of what it means to have integrity and character? What are some of the characteristics that make them the way they are?

Why do you think that trust is important in a friendship or relationship?

After reading Philippians 4:8 again, what are some things you can do to constantly think this way?

Thursday

For your weekly challenge, you will spend some time studying the fruit of the Spirit as you try to implement all nine character traits in your life.

For each characteristic, think of a way you can demonstrate that fruit to someone in the next few days. For example, when it comes to peace, you might have a friend at school that you argue with constantly. Your plan might be to create peace by not arguing with them the next time a conflict starts, and by keeping yourself from getting angry. The hope will be that your focus on peace will change the tone of the argument and cause the other person not to get as angry, too. These need to be random acts of love, joy, peace, etc. that 1) does not draw attention to you (think subtle) and 2) are aimed at someone who you are not already treating in this way (in other words, showing love to a boy/girl friend is great but does not count for this challenge).

Love:

Joy:

Peace:

Patience:

Kindness:

Goodness:

Faithfulness:

Gentleness:

Self-control:

Weekend Review

Spend time this weekend reviewing this week's lesson and your answers to the questions.

Optional weekend reading: Mark 8

WEEK EIGHT NOTES:

Know how to be healthy and
WEEK NINE
why you need to stay that way

Do you not know that your bodies are temples of the Holy Spirit, who is in you, whom you have received from God? You are not your own; you were bought at a price. Therefore honor God with your bodies.1 Corinthians 6:19-20

Monday

As mentioned in the introduction of this book, the term "Freshman 15" refers to the 15 pounds a college freshman gains that first year away from home. The reason for this is that the student leaves everything from accountability to home cooked meals and begins to stay up all night and eat unhealthily. The question is not really how that happens but why is this important. First, it matters because basic science tells us that you will make better grades if you get enough sleep, exercise, and eat right. Secondly, according to the

Bible, your body is the temple of the Holy Spirit. In 1 Corinthians 6:19-20, we see that God lives in you, and you are instructed to treat your body as you would if you had Jesus as a guest in your home. If you are like most people, you probably had to help clean your house before someone came over. In the same way, you should remember that the Holy Spirit lives in you, and you are instructed to honor God by keeping your body healthy.

The truth is, everything that you do has a spiritual benefit or consequence because you are a spiritual being. You were made by God, and as a Christian, you have the Holy Spirit living in you. In 3 John 1:2 we read, "Dear friend, I pray that you may enjoy good health and that all may go well with you, even as your soul is getting along well." This verse reminds us that our health directly affects our soul and spirit. When someone becomes lazy, it affects what they do and how they live for God. When someone is in good shape, they have the endurance to go, do, and be the hands and feet of Jesus. It's all connected, so you must learn how to be healthy.

Let's look at your health in three parts: body, mind and spirit. How can you make your body more healthy? The answer is to get in shape and watch what you eat. Secondly, how do you make your mind healthy? This starts with getting enough sleep and keeping yourself from undue stress. This can help keep you from getting sick, which can cause even more health problems. Finally, how do you keep a healthy spirit? This starts by gaining maturity in your faith, then you live it out every day of your life. Everything you do should be for the benefit of your relationship with Jesus. 1 Corinthians 10:31 says, "So whether you eat or drink or whatever you do, do it all for the glory of God." Your body, mind, and spirit are all connected. Keep them healthy, and you will see an overall wellness in your life, faith, relationships, body, and mind.

Tuesday

Even though none of her college friends knew this, Emma has struggled with her weight since she was 10 years old. She used to starve herself by pretending to eat lunch at school and then complain of being too-full for dinner. She felt better about herself when she was skinny and even liked the attention she would get from the boys in high school. By the time she got to college, her unhealthy eating was such a pattern that she almost did it automatically. Along with not eating enough, Emma was not getting enough sleep, which affected everything that she did. She also had to visit the campus medical center a few times that first semester because she was always getting sick. Eventually the doctor told her that she was sick because she wasn't taking good care of yourself. Emma decided to talk to Nora about it, and Nora offered to help. Nora told her that she was not going to get fat by eating healthy, but that healthy food and regular exercise was going to give her more energy and help her to feel better. The two started running together and committed to being open to each other about their health issues. Emma started to feel better soon after, and most importantly, she began to feel good about herself and committed her body, mind, and spirit to the Lord.

Fill in the blank as you learn this verse this week:

Do you not know that your _____ are _____ of the Holy _____, who is ___ you, whom you have _____ from God? You are ___ your ____; you were bought at a _____. Therefore _____ God with your _____.1 Corinthians 6:19-20

Spend some time in prayer about your health, asking God to give you the knowledge and courage to pursue a healthy body, mind, and spirit.

Wednesday

Fill in the blank to complete this verse

Do you _____ know that your _____ are _____ of the _____ _____, who is in _____, whom you have _____ from _____? You are ___ your ____; you were _____ at a _____. Therefore _____ _____ with your _____. __ Corinthians _____:19-20

In your own words, why is it important in your relationship with God to be physically healthy?

What were some healthy habits that you had in high school that you have not continued in college?

Which part of you is more healthy and unhealthy: Body, Mind, Spirit? Why?

Name 3 things that you can start doing now to be more healthy in body, mind, and spirit.

Thursday

For your weekly challenge, take the three healthy choices that you listed in the last question yesterday and create a plan for them. For example, if your goal is to start exercising by biking, your plan might be to start riding your bike for one hour, three days a week after your last class. Your plan needs to be specific and realistic.

Healthy Choice #1:

My Specific Plan:

Healthy Choice #2:

My Specific Plan:

Healthy Choice #3:

My Specific Plan:

Weekend Review

Spend time this weekend reviewing this week's lesson and your answers to the questions.

Optional weekend reading: Mark 9

WEEK NINE NOTES:

Know how to be a good student
WEEK TEN
and stay in school

All hard work brings a profit, but mere talk leads only to poverty. Proverbs 14:23

Monday

When I was in college, I would always say that college would be amazing if it wasn't for the academics. Even though taking classes is the reason you are in college, it often seems like the one thing holding you back from having the best time of your life. The fact is, if you do not put enough effort on making good grades, you will not be in college for long, and all of the social advantages will be gone as well. The smart thing to do is to learn how to be a good college student, so that you can remain in college. Proverbs 14:23 tells us that there is a positive benefit to working hard. This verse is true about a lot of things but is certainly applicable to doing well in school.

By this time in your freshman year, you have already taken some tests and made some grades. You know what the college routine feels like and how the college classroom experience relates to that of high school. Are you making good grades? Are your college grades better or worse than your high school grades? These are important questions to ask. You may be wondering how being a good student relates to your faith. Think back to one of the verses we learned last week; as 1 Corinthians 10:31 says, "So whether you eat or drink or whatever you do, do it all for the glory of God." Just like with your health and relationships, you should honor the Lord with your mind and your academic achievements.

If you are still struggling to find your way in becoming a good college student, let me give you some verses of Scripture that might help.

1. *Dedicate your academics to the Lord*: And whatever you do, whether in word or deed, do it all in the name of the Lord Jesus, giving thanks to God the Father through him. Colossians 3:17

2. *Set goals to be a good student:* I press on toward the goal for the prize of the upward call of God in Christ Jesus. Philippians 3:14

3. *Work hard to reach your academic goals:* Be diligent to present yourself approved to God as a workman who does not need to be ashamed, accurately handling the word of truth. 2 Timothy 2:15

Tuesday

JT and Emma have History 101 together on Tuesdays and Thursdays at 1:00 PM. Emma is a better note taker than JT, but he is more interested in history than she is. They make good study partners, especially with the upcoming history mid-term exam that is worth half of their overall grade. The plan was to study alone each night and then come together the weekend before the test and spend all of Sunday afternoon talking through the chapters. When they met up at the library for the big study session, JT wasn't prepared. He had not looked over the material enough which meant that he didn't know enough about the content to pull his weight in the review conversation. This made Emma frustrated, and she let JT know it. He admitted that he should have been more prepared but confessed that high school was easier for him and that he struggled to write down all that was said during the professor's weekly lectures. What he realized in that moment was that coasting through high school did not prepare him to be a good college student, and yet he needed a good grade on this test to keep his scholarship. Emma committed to help him study for this test and then later to give him some tips on how to be a better note-taker in class.

Fill in the blank as you learn this verse this week:

All _____ _____ brings a _____, but mere _____ leads only to _____. _____ 14:23

Spend some time in prayer asking the Lord to remove distractions that might keep you from making good grades.

Wednesday

Fill in the blank to complete this verse

All _____ _____ brings a _____, but _____ _____ _____ only to _____.

_____ 14:_____

What are some of the main differences you have noticed about being a student in high school and in college?

What are some of the common distractions that make it hard to study in college?

What study skills are needed to make good grades in college?

How does Colossians 3:17 change the way you view studying and making good grades?

Thursday

The challenge for the week is to make a list of ten new ideas that would help you be a better student. For example, if your biggest distraction is that you have a hard time concentrating in your dorm room because of the noise, you might think of a couple new places you can go to study. If your biggest issue is scheduling time to study each day, you should focus on making a list of ways to help with that. Take the time and make sure this list helps you make changes before you get further along in college. If you can not think of ten things, have a brainstorming session with a fellow student or a professor.

Weekend Review

Spend time this weekend reviewing this week's lesson and your answers to the questions.

Optional weekend reading: Mark 10

WEEK TEN NOTES:

WEEK ELEVEN

For which of you, desiring to build a tower, does not first sit down and count the cost, whether he has enough to complete it? Luke 14:28

Monday

There are many differences between high school and college, from living with a roommate to only going to a class a few times a week. But, by now you might have realized that one of the biggest changes is having to manage your time and money by yourself. Some students are fortunate to have come from a home where those tasks were shared as you got older, allowing you to learn how to handle these important responsibilities at home. For others, this was not the case; and therefore, managing time and money in college might prove to be a major struggle.

Learning to manage your time and money are both adult tasks that anyone on his/her own must get a handle on. The older you get, the more responsibilities you will have to keep up with; and the better job you do at life management, the more successful your life will be. In Luke 14:28, Jesus asks an interesting question when he said, "For which of you, desiring to build a tower, does not first sit down and count the cost, whether he has enough to complete it?" In other words, how will you reach a goal if you have not planned out all the steps? How will you get a degree if you forget to meet with your advisor or fail to remember an important assignment due date? How can you stay healthy if you spend all your of money on entertainment and do not have enough to buy food? You can not be careless with your important responsibilities, now that you are on your own.

The way to ensure that you handle your time and money wisely is to commit it to the Lord. In Ephesians 5:15-16 we read: "Look carefully then how you walk, not as unwise but as wise, making the best use of the time, because the days are evil." This verse is a warning not to waste the time (& money) that you have been given, or you might lose it. A key word for you to learn is stewardship, which means being responsible for the resources you have been given. Time and money are two of your greatest resources. Manage them wisely as you learn to become a good steward by honoring the Lord with the time and money you have been given.

Tuesday

Emma was walking to the Cafe for dinner when she met up with Sam, who was going in at the same time. He looked like something was bothering him, so Emma asked him what was wrong. He said that he was afraid that he might fail his 8:00 AM class because of too many absences. He added that, even though he had a high B in the class, he missed too many classes and was expecting to fail the class. She looked at him with a confused look and asked why he missed that class so much. He admitted to her that he had a hard time waking up early and accidentally slept through the class five times. He added that, according to the syllabus, over four absences would result in an automatic F in the class. He couldn't believe that he had been so irresponsible by letting this happen. Emma asked him if he had missed any other classes and discovered that he had, as well as an interview for an on-campus job last week. Emma knew that Sam was committed to school, so she wondered if he was just really bad at time management. She offered to help him and suggested that he start by making a schedule of his week, so that he could see his week at a glance. Then, he would need to get someone to help keep him accountable for sticking to it. They sat down and charted out his class schedule, time for studying, a reasonable bed time, and made sure he had enough down time. Then she told him that she would call him every morning at 7AM, for the next two weeks, to make sure he was awake. Hopefully, that would help him keep up with all that he needs to do for the rest of the semester. Now, he just needed to beg his professor to give him one more chance before failing him for too many absences.

Fill in the blank as you learn this verse this week:

For which of you, _____ to build a _____,
does not first sit down and _____ the _____,
whether he has _____ to complete it? Luke
14:28

Spend some time in prayer, thinking about how to be
responsible with the resources that you have been
given.

Wednesday

Fill in the blank to complete this verse

For _____ of you, _____ to _____ a _____, does not first _____ _____ and _____ the _____, whether he has _____ to _____ it? _____ ____:_____

How would you describe your time management skills in high school and now in college?

How would you describe your money management skills in high school and now in college?

What are some obstacles that might keep you from being a good time and/or money manager?

What does it mean for you to be a good steward of the resources that you have been given?

Thursday

For this week's challenge, you need to find a blank weekly calendar online, print it out, and outline your typical week. Start by putting in your class and work schedule and any other weekly events that you know of. Secondly, decide when you will study, eat, and spend time working through this devotional book. Schedule when you will wake up and go to sleep, and then fill in the extra time with activities that you enjoy. Be honest and make a commitment to stick to it.

The second part of the assignment is to make a monthly budget. At the top, put the amount of money you get (or make) in a month. List your estimated expenses, starting from the most important down to the insignificant. If you run out of money before you finish listing your expenses, you will need to reduce or remove some things. Just like with your schedule, be sure to stick to this budget so that you have the money to afford the important things in your life.

Weekend Review

Spend time this weekend reviewing this week's lesson and your answers to the questions.

Optional weekend reading: Mark 11

WEEK ELEVEN NOTES:

WEEK TWELVE

and how to be datable

*So flee youthful passions and pursue righteousness,
faith, love, and peace, along with those who call on
the Lord from a pure heart. 2 Timothy 2:22*

Monday

If you haven't noticed yet, dating in college is
different than in high school. In some ways, it's more
laid back. In high school, dates are official events
when you ask/get asked out, go to pick them up/ get
picked up, and then dropped back home before curfew.
In college, people hang out more, and even when there
is a more formal date night, it wraps up on campus
where you both already live.

Not only is the process of dating different in
college, the attitude toward dating is different because
you are older and you have more freedom, which
means you must be more mature. 2 Timothy 2:22
encourages you to grow up and pursue love,

righteousness, faith, and peace with a pure heart. You are an adult now; therefore, if you are going to take on the responsibility of dating someone as a young adult, you must step into that role with maturity and a pure heart.

Here is one rule to remember when it comes to dating: whoever you go out with is (most likely) someone's future spouse. In other words, most people get married, and the person you date will one day be married. They might marry you, but you will not know for sure until your wedding day. So, with that in mind, you need to treat that person in the same way that you hope someone else is treating your future spouse.

Here are a few Bible verses that can help you put that in perspective:

Flee from sexual immorality. Every other sin a person commits is outside the body, but the sexually immoral person sins against his own body. 1 Corinthians 6:18

Love is patient, love is kind. It does not envy, it does not boast, it is not proud. It does not dishonor others, it is not self-seeking, it is not easily angered, it keeps no record of wrongs. Love does not delight in evil but rejoices with the truth. It always protects, always trusts, always hopes, always perseveres. Love never fails. 1 Corinthians 13:4-8a

Let no one despise you for your youth, but set the believers an example in speech, in conduct, in love, in faith, in purity. 1 Timothy 4:12

Delight yourself in the Lord, and he will give you the desires of your heart. Psalm 37:4

Tuesday

Every since he first saw her, Chase has wanted to ask Nora out. As their friendship developed, he became afraid that asking her out might ruin the friend relationship that they had. Chase had dated girls in high school but had never felt like this about a girl before. He liked those girls in high school, but he thinks he might be falling in love with Nora. The best part about their relationship is that they started as friends. They have hung out dozens of times, and he already knows so much about her. Even though he is not sure if she feels the same, he is willing to ask her out on a date and find out. So he does, and she accepts. Fast forward a few months and Chase and Nora are in a serious dating relationship. Their relationship is healthy because it was built upon a friendship that was based on Jesus. Their relationship is pure because they value one another enough to keep it that way. Their relationship is promising because they have the support of their friends, and they are open about their feelings, hopes, and dreams for their future.

Fill in the blank as you learn this verse this week:

So _____ youthful _____ and pursue
_____, faith, _____, and peace, along with those
who _____ on the Lord from a _____ _____.
2 Timothy __:22

Spend some time in prayer about your current and/or
future serious relationships. Pray for the person that
you will one day marry, and pray for the person who
might be currently dating your future spouse.

Wednesday

Fill in the blank to complete this verse

So _____ _____ _____ and pursue
_____, _____, _____, and _____, along
with those who _____ on the _____ from a
_____ _____.
2 _____ ____:_____

What are the differences you have observed in dating
in high school and in college?

What words would you use to describe a serious dating
relationship in college?

How might the following situations damage a serous dating relationship?

Poor communication:

Sleeping together:

Dating other people:

Fighting all the time:

Who is a couple that you know that have a good dating relationship? What do you like most about their relationship?

Thursday

The challenge for this week is to create a list of non-negotiables for dating. A non-negotiable is a commitment you make with yourself about something that, under no circumstances, you will ever do. For example, as someone who tries to honor God with my body, a non-negotiable might be: "Under no circumstances will I ever use illicit drugs." That means that I have made this commitment. I might then share it with a few friends that can keep me accountable. When it comes to dating, your non-negotiables need to center around sexual purity, faithfulness, and balancing time with this person and all the other important things you need (studying, sleep, other friendships, etc).

Below is a place to write your non-negotiables and to put the name of one person who will keep you accountable for it. I have given you three topics and then a fourth blank for you to come up with one. If you are not currently dating someone (which most people reading this probably aren't), you need to make this commitment for the future and put as your accountability partner a general person like "roommate", "friend", "college minister", etc.

Non-negotiable #1 - Sexual Purity

Under no circumstances will I:

Accountability Partner:

Non-negotiable #2 - Faithfulness in Relationship

Under no circumstances will I:

Accountability Partner:

Non-negotiable #3 - Balancing Time

Under no circumstances will I:

Accountability Partner:

Non-negotiable #4 -

Under no circumstances will I:

Accountability Partner:

Weekend Review

Spend time this weekend reviewing this week's lesson and your answers to the questions.

Optional weekend reading: Mark 12

WEEK TWELVE NOTES:

But seek first the kingdom of God and his righteousness, and all these things will be added to you. Matthew 6:33

Monday

A few weeks ago we talked about managing your time and money. These are important things to learn at your age, but the greater responsibility than life management is life balance. You will never find contentment in your life without balance. Too much of anything is never going to be a good thing. If you have a job that takes all of your time and you never have time to rest, you will wear yourself down. If you always spend more money than you make, you will never find financial freedom from debt. If you don't spend the time developing your relationships (beginning with your relationship with Christ), you will never reach the depth of intimacy that is the essence of life. Balance in life is critical to your well-being and your future development as a person.

The first step in finding balance is determining a perspective of what is most important to you. Matthew 6:33 gives us a clue of how this works. According to Jesus, we should seek the kingdom of the Lord and His righteousness first, then all other things will fall into place. This verse helps us to see that our life should be built on our foundation of our faith. Some people think of their life as a pie chart, with their faith as a section of the pie. Some might see their walk with Christ as a large piece or maybe an even section as it relates to the others. Instead of a pie chart, I want you to think of your faith as your core, with all other aspects of life branching off from there. This way, if you focus on keeping your relationship with Jesus healthy, all other parts of your life will potentially be healthy as well.

The second step to finding balance in your life is to even out the weights of the other aspects of your life. Think about one of those old balance scales that have to be evenly weighted to balance. As you think about your life, you should try to balance work with play, activity with rest, and saving with spending. There will always be seasons of time when this is not possible, like during exam week for example, but overall you should look to stay balanced on the scale of your life.

The third step to finding balance in your life is to learn to say "no" to the things that aren't important. Once you find balance, you will need to work to keep things in balance. Saying "no" is important as you use wisdom in your planning. No one can be healthy who constantly lives out of balance. Take to heart the words of 2 Peter 3:17 that says, "You therefore, beloved, knowing this beforehand, take care that you are not carried away with the error of lawless people and lose your own stability." Balance equals stability and gives you the best chance at living your life fully and faithfully.

Tuesday

Every Tuesday night, Chase, Sam, JT, Nora, and Emma all go to a Bible study sponsored by the campus ministry. This has been an important part of their lives and has become the foundation of their relationships with each other. One night after a time of worship and listening to a speaker, the group divided up into their small groups and were given a task to help find balance in life. Their assignment was to make a list of the things they do and how much time they spend doing it. They laughed as they tried to think of all the things they spend their time doing. Sam spent way too much time playing his X-Box, and Chase and Nora spent a lot of time each day together doing nothing, as Emma noted. It was also determined that JT didn't get enough sleep, usually only about four hours a night, and the whole group made fun of Emma for saying that she actually spent about twenty hours a week studying in the library. This was a fun assignment that taught these friends the importance of balance in life. They vowed to help each other be more well-rounded as they all had things they could work on.

Fill in the blank as you learn this verse this week:

But _____ first the _____ of _____ and his _____, and all these _____ will be _____ to you. _____ 6:33

Spend some time in prayer about seeking to go deeper in your relationship with your Savior and then finding balance in the other parts of your life.

Wednesday

Fill in the blank to complete this verse

But _____ _____ the _____ of
_____ and his _____, and _____ these
_____ will be _____ to _____.
_____ ___:_____

Why is it important to find balance in your life now
while you are in college?

What are some ways you can seek first the kingdom of
God before any other part of your life?

Make a list of the things in your life that are out of balance.

List your priorities in your life right now from most important to least important.

Thursday

Just like our friends in their Tuesday night small group, this week's challenge is to find balance in the things you do in life. You have 168 hours in your week. In the spaces below, list the hours you spend in each of the categories for a typical week. Then, look back at each one and make sure you are spending the right amount of time and finding overall balance. You might need to play with the numbers afterwards to re-adjust and re-balance. I know this might be hard for most people. These are all estimations but should be as realistic as possible.

Sleeping: _____

In Class: _____

Studying outside of class: _____

Eating: _____

Getting dressed / Going to bed: _____

Praying, reading the Bible/devotional: _____

Time in worship and discipleship: _____

Exercising: _____

Working in a job/volunteer responsibilities: _____

Spending time with friend group A: _____

Spending time with friend group B: _____

Spending time with friend group C: _____

Spending time with friend group D: _____

Traveling/Running Errands: _____

Time alone/Hobby: _____

Meetings/Appointments: _____

Other: _____

Total Hours: _____ (168 maximum)

Questions:

What do you spend the most time doing?

What do you spend the least time doing?

How does that compare to your list of priorities you made on the last question yesterday?

What needs to be tweaked? What needs to be totally re-balanced?

Weekend Review

Spend time this weekend reviewing this week's lesson and your answers to the questions.

Optional weekend reading: Mark 13

WEEK THIRTEEN NOTES:

"You are the light of the world. A city set on a hill cannot be hidden." Matthew 5:14

Monday

What does leadership mean to you? Go ahead and think of your answer before you continue reading. Leadership is a broad term that can represent a specific role or a general theme. This week, I want to give you a definition of leadership that will change the way you live and relate to others.

I believe that every follower of Jesus has the same baseline calling. Everyone, regardless of how old or how mature they are in their faith, starts with the same calling from God. That calling is found in Matthew 5:14. During Jesus' sermon on the mountain, He said, "You are the light of the world. A city set on a hill cannot be hidden." That is what you are called to be: light. Not only are you called to be light, you are called to be the light of the world and such a bright light that you can be compared to a city shining on the top of a hill. That is leadership.

When a group of people are walking in the darkness, the person who is holding the flashlight will naturally become the leader. The light will serve as a source of vision to show everyone the way. The same can be true about those who are following Jesus. As Psalm 119:105 states, the Word of God is a "lamp unto my feet, and a light unto my path."

When you are the light of the world, you are leading people toward Jesus and away from the world. You become a leader of light in the following three ways:

1) Through the way you act. If you are committed to being a light, you will act more like the leader you have become. If you have ever been in a leadership position in school or in a group, the moment you realized you were the leader, you probably sat up a little taller and began to act more responsible. When you understand the potential of being a light in your world, you will need to step up to the role of a leader.

2) Through the words you say. As you begin to act differently, you will also begin to speak differently. A leader who is reading God's Word knows the truth and will speak out against falsehoods. When someone is hurting, the leader will naturally have words to comfort them. When someone is feeling lost, leaders will be able to speak truth into them by shining a light on their path.

3) Through the difference you make. As a leader and a light, you will stick out and be noticed. Just like a city on a hill top shining light in darkness, you will be making an impact through your witness and your ability to shine. That is what it means to be a light. That is what it looks like to be a leader. Now go and shine your light so that everyone around you will know the Lord, your God.

Tuesday

Emma was sitting in her class waiting on it to start when the girl sitting next to her looked like she had been crying. Emma had talked with this classmate before but did not feel that she really knew her at all. She was concerned though, so she asked if she was okay. The girl shook her head to say yes, but then class started so nothing else was said. After class, Emma caught up with the girl and asked again if she needed to talk. That is when the girl introduced herself as Jules and began to tell Emma about how her friends had stood her up for lunch and then lied about what they were doing. Emma understood how upsetting that would be and began to talk to her about true friendship, faith, and forgiveness. She shared a verse that she had recently learned about and immediately made Jules feel better. Then Jules surprised Emma by telling her how she knew that Emma was a Christian and how she could tell that there was something different about her. Jules then mentioned other examples that she had noticed when Emma treated other people with love and compassion. Emma was surprised that Jules had even noticed her, much less remembered those situations. That instance reminded

149

Emma that other people are watching and noticing how she acts as a Christian. She will either represent Jesus accurately through her love for others, or she will misrepresent Him by not living as she should. Either way, she is a leader.

Fill in the blank as you learn this verse this week:

"You are the _____ of the _____. A _____ set on a hill cannot be _____." _____
___:___

Spend some time in prayer, asking God to give you opportunities to be His light in your world.

Wednesday

Fill in the blank to complete this verse

"You _____ _____ _____ of the _____. ___
_____ __ on a _____ _____ be _____."
_____ ___:____

What does it mean to you to be the light of your world?

Read all of Matthew 5:14-16. How can a Christian cover his/her light in college?

How does it make you feel to think that others are watching how you act and noticing when you shine your light brightly on others?

In what ways, and with which people, can you be a light in your world at college?

Thursday

This week's challenge is to be a light in your world. For the next week, I want you to wake up and read Matthew 5:14-16 until you know it by heart. Then you will be looking for ways to shine your light so others can see Jesus. In the spaces below, record at least one example per day for the next week of when you were able to be God's light to others. Then, I recommend you re-read those examples every time you need some encouragement to uncover your light and shine brightly.

Thursday:

Friday:

Saturday:

Sunday:

Monday:

Tuesday:

Wednesday:

Weekend Review

Spend time this weekend reviewing this week's lesson and your answers to the questions.

Optional weekend reading: Mark 14

WEEK FOURTEEN NOTES:

Know how to continue growing and

WEEK FIFTEEN

why that is critical to your life

*I pray that out of his glorious riches he may strengthen
you with power through his Spirit in your inner
being, so that Christ may dwell in your hearts through
faith. And I pray that you, being rooted and
established in love. Ephesians 3:16-17*

Monday

There is a verse that I learned in college that was so
important to me then and still is to this day. It is found
in Philippians 1:6 and says, "being confident of this,
that he who began a good work in you will carry it on
to completion until the day of Christ Jesus." When I
was in college, this verse was a confirmation that, even
though I was a work-in-progress, I was a good work,
and someone that Jesus wasn't going to give up on.
The same is true with you. You are a good work, and
He will carry you through to completion as long as
you live. That is a promise and a challenge to keep

growing, keep learning, and keep following Jesus closely.

For the past 15 weeks, you have been learning how to be a follower of Jesus as a college student. My hope is that you have learned what it means to be authentic about your faith as you live consistent with God's Word. As Ephesians 3:16-17 says, I hope that you will allow Jesus to strengthen you with His power so that Christ can live through you. I pray, as Paul did, that you would be rooted in the love of your Savior as you shine His light on others.

Here are some final thoughts and scripture as you close out your first semester of college.

Lean on your Bible as your guide in all matters:
Let the Word of Christ richly dwell within you, with all wisdom teaching and admonishing one another with psalms and hymns and spiritual songs, singing with thankfulness in your hearts to God. Colossians 3:16

You are an adult now so start living like one:
When I was a child, I used to speak like a child, think like a child, reason like a child; when I became a man, I did away with childish things. 1 Corinthians 13:11

Pursue a mature faith that is ready to change the world around you:
Therefore leaving the elementary teaching about the Christ, let us press on to maturity, not laying again a foundation of repentance from dead works and of faith toward God. Hebrews 6:1-2

Never stop growing in your walk with Christ:
But grow in the grace and knowledge of our Lord and Savior Jesus Christ To Him be the glory, both now and to the day of eternity. Amen. 2 Peter 3:18

Tuesday

Chase, Nora, Sam, Emma, and JT are almost finished with their first semester of their freshman year in college. They have done pretty well in their classes and have learned even more outside the classroom about life, relationships, and how to live out their faith in college. It hasn't been a perfect ride for any of them, but it has been filled with moments of growth and maturity. For all five of them, the most important thing has been the community they formed together. None of them can imagine what this semester would have been like without their friendships. Now they will all go their separate ways for the holidays, with plans to visit one another after Christmas. The challenge for all of them is how to keep this momentum going into the spring of next year. They know that their schedules will be different and other opportunities will come around, but they are sure that they need to stick together and keep meeting and growing as a team. At their last campus ministry event for the semester, they were encouraged with Hebrews 10:24-25 which says, "And let us consider how we may spur one another on toward love and good deeds, not giving up meeting together, as some are in the habit of doing, but encouraging one another—and all the more as you see the Day approaching." This is their group motto and theme. We all need Christ and each other, and that is a valuable lesson learned in the past few months by JT, Emma, Nora, Sam, and Chase.

Fill in the blank as you learn this verse this week:

I pray that out of his _____ _____ he may _____ you with power through his _____ in your inner being, so that Christ may _____ in your hearts through _____. And I pray that you, being _____ and _____ in _____.
Ephesians ___:16-17

Wednesday

Fill in the blanks to complete this verse

I _____ that _____ of his _____
_____ he may _____ you with
_____ through his _____ in your _____
_____, so that _____ may _____ in
your _____ through _____. And I pray
that you, being _____ and _____
in _____. _____ ___:___ — _____

What have you learned this semester about yourself
and your relationship with Jesus?

Name three things you wish you had known about yourself before starting college?

What is your plan for continuing to grow in your faith now that you have completed this book?

What did you learn about habits of personal discipleship from this book?

Thursday

For your last Thursday challenge, you are to outline your plan for continuing this weekly devotional habit now that you are finished with this book. What will you read or listen to each day? How will you continue to memorize Scripture like I have encouraged you to do with the fill-in-the-blanks? Will you break it up in weekly themes, or will you study something different each day? In the space below, describe how you will keep this momentum of growth, both during the holidays and during your next semester of school.

Many blessings to you. May you forever be rooted and established in Christ's love. Amen.

Weekend Review

Spend time this weekend reviewing this week's lesson and your answers to the questions.

Optional weekend reading: Mark 15
Next week, finish Mark by reading chapter 16

WEEK FIFTEEN NOTES:

ADDITIONAL NOTES

Other book & resources by Tommy McGregor & TheTransMission

Lost in Transition: Becoming Spiritually Prepared For College

This book helps graduating students know who they are, understand the environment they are going to, and learn how to be themselves in that new setting. The 3rd edition includes a full study guide and added content.

Senior Summit Online Video Series

The Senior Summit is a video series created for seniors, including interviews from experts on the transition to college.

The Freedom Permit: Creating A Vision of Discipleship For Your Senior's Last Year in High School

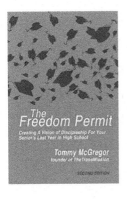

The Freedom Permit is a book for parents of high school seniors to help them maximize this last year in high school. The book focuses on four transitional topics: faith development, life management, social behaviors, and goal setting.

Ownership Road: Leading Our Children To An Authentic Faith That Prepares Them For Life After High School

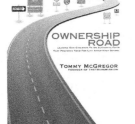

This is a book for parents of younger kids (ages 5-15) to help them understand how to raise their children with those post-high school challenges in mind.

Ownership RoadMap: A Personal Study Guide For Ownership

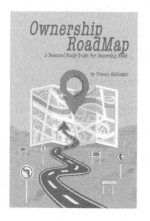

This book was created to be a partner to Ownership Road and is intended to serve as a personal study guide for parents reading through the book, either within a small group or on their own.

For more information on these books and online resources, go to the links below.

TheTransMission: www.thetransmission.org

TDR Publishing :   www.transitioncentral.net

More About TheTransMisison:

Founded in 2010 by Tommy McGregor, TheTransMission trains leaders, equips parents, and prepares students for the transition to life after high school. Through providing resources and transition coaching, TheTransMission is one of the leading voices in the country for this critical topic.

More About The Author:

Tommy McGregor is an author, speaker, ministry coach and the founder of TheTransMission. He has spent over two decades in ministry working with teenagers, parents, and ministry leaders, and is passionate about helping others develop a sense of who God has created them to be. Visit Tommy on his blog at www.tommymcgregor.com.

Made in the USA
Columbia, SC
05 June 2019